Kindergarten

Jumbo Workbook

This workbook belongs to

....

Use pencils, crayons, and stickers to complete the activities in this book. When there is a sticker missing, you will see this pattern:

Dear Parents,

Welcome to the *Jumbo Kindergarten Workbook*!

Here are some tips to help ensure that your child gets the most from this book.

★ Look at the pages with your child, ensuring he or she knows what to do before starting.

★ Plan short, regular sessions, only doing one or two pages at a time.

★ Praise your child's efforts and improvements.

★ Encourage your child to assess his or her own efforts in a positive way. For example, say: "You've written some great A's there. Which one do you think you did best?"

★ Make the learning sessions positive experiences. Give prompts where they might help. If a section is too hard for your child, leave those pages until he or she is ready for them.

★ Relate the learning to things in your child's world. For example, if your child is working on a page about the color red, ask him or her to find some red things in your home.

★ There are stickers to use throughout the book. They help build your child's hand-eye coordination and observation skills. Encourage your child to place the stickers on each page before starting the other activities.

Together, the activities in the workbook help build a solid understanding of early learning concepts to ensure your child is ready for first grade.

We wish your child hours of enjoyment with this fun workbook!

Scholastic Early Learning

Contents

Trace the uppercase and lowercase **a**'s.

Aa Aa Aa Aa Aa

Adam ate an apple.

Check the words that start with **a**.

☑ **ant**

☐ **crab**

☐ **lamp**

☐ **alligator**

☐ **anchor**

☐ **orange**

Trace the uppercase and lowercase **b**'s.

Bb Bb Bb Bb Bb

Bella bought a bow.

Find and circle six **b**'s.

b d   b   h

   p   h   P

      b

   d   p   d

      p   d

         p   b

h   b   h

Trace the uppercase and lowercase **c**'s.

Cc Cc Cc Cc

Cody can cook.

Write the **c**'s in these words.

camel

o___topus

ro___ket

lo___k

___at

du___k

Trace the uppercase and lowercase **d**'s.

Dd Dd Dd Dd

Dora drew a dog.

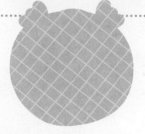

Draw lines from the **d** to the words that have a **d** in them.

sandals

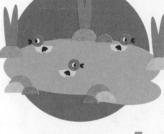

pond

truck

d

donkey

daisy

Trace the uppercase and lowercase **e**'s.

Ee Ee Ee Ee

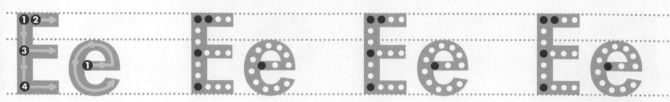

Ella met an elephant.

Follow the **e**'s to lead **E**ddie to the **exit**.

Start → e	f	d	f	d
f	e	e	e	g	d
f c	d	f	d	e	g f
c e	e	e	e	
g e	d	f	d	c	EXIT
f e	d	f	c	f	
g e	e	e	e	→ Finish

Trace the uppercase and lowercase f's.

Ff Ff Ff Ff Ff

Finn found a flower.

Find and circle six f's.

Trace the uppercase and lowercase **g**'s.

Gg Gg Gg Gg

Gabby got glasses.

Write the **g**'s in these words.

pi___

mu___

fla___

Trace the uppercase and lowercase **h**'s.

Hh Hh Hh Hh

Harry has a hat.

Find and circle three **h**'s.

b h d b d h h d

Trace the uppercase and lowercase i's.

Ii Ii Ii Ii Ii Ii Ii Ii

Iris likes ice cream.

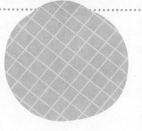

Color the boxes with lowercase i's in **blue**.
Color the boxes with uppercase I's in green.

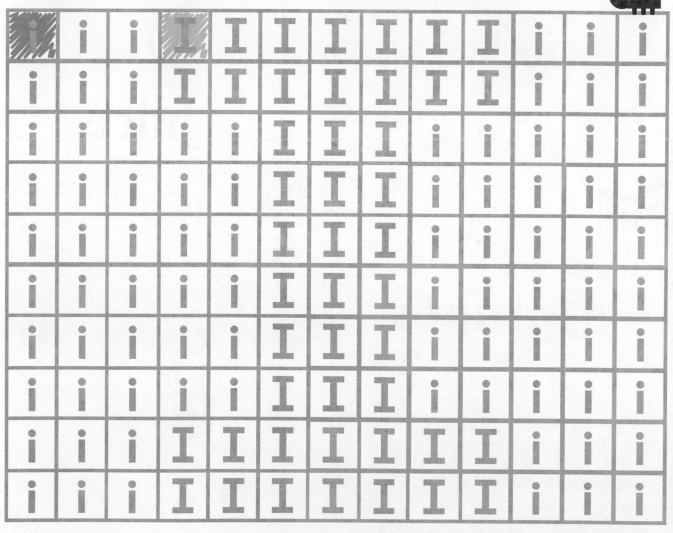

Trace the uppercase and lowercase **j**'s.

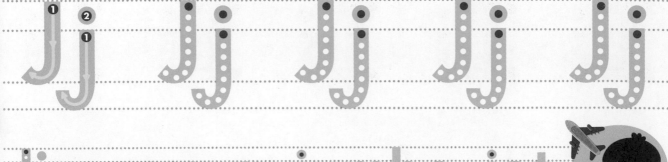

Jim saw a jumbo jet.

Check the words that start with **j**.

☐ **jewel**

☐ **juice**

☐ **grapes**

☐ **jacket**

☐ **jeans**

☐ **insect**

Trace the uppercase and lowercase **k**'s.

Kk Kk Kk Kk

Kiki has a kitten.

Draw lines from the **k** to the words that have a **k** in them.

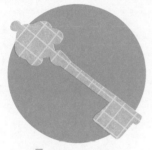

key

bike

koala

k

book

tiger

Trace the uppercase and lowercase l's.

Ll Ll Ll Ll Ll Ll Ll

Luke likes lollipops.

Follow the l's to lead the lion to its lunch.

Start →

l	l	l	k	m	k
m	n	l	n	k	m
mn	k	o	l	n	mo
o	l	l	l	k	l k
m	l	o	n	k	o mm
n	l	l	l	m	m
m	n	o	l	l	

→ Finish

Trace the uppercase and lowercase **m**'s.

Mm Mm Mm

Milly drinks milk.

Check the words that start with **m**.

☐ nest ☐ mask ☐ moon

Trace the uppercase and lowercase **n**'s.

Nn Nn Nn Nn

Nina saved a newt.

Draw lines from the **n** to the words that have an **n** in them.

 hen one

 **n**

 brick train

Trace the uppercase and lowercase **o**'s.

O o O o O o O o O o

Otto ate an orange.

Write the **o**'s in these words.

w___lf

b___x

fr___g

___range

igl___

ball___n

Trace the uppercase and lowercase p's.

Pp Pp Pp Pp Pp

Pete has a pet parrot.

Check the words that start with p.

☐ penguin

☐ ball

☐ pie

☐ pony

☐ potato

☐ dog

Trace the uppercase and lowercase **q**'s.

Qq Qq Qq Qq

Quinn can run quickly.

Check the words that start with **q**.

☐kite   ☐**quilt**   ☐queen

Trace the uppercase and lowercase **r**'s.

Rr Rr Rr Rr Rr

Rob wears red socks.

Find and circle three **r**'s.

c n s r

r r c s

Trace the uppercase and lowercase **s**'s.

Susan is six.

Color the boxes with lowercase **s**'s in **yellow**.
Color the boxes with uppercase **S**'s in **blue**.

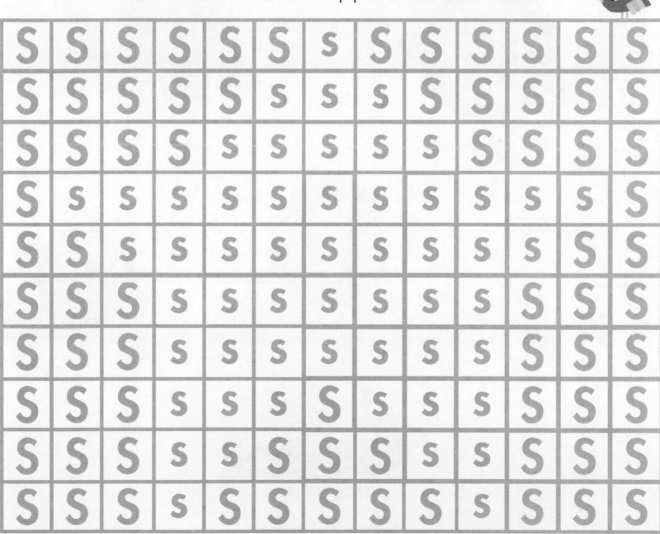

Trace the uppercase and lowercase t's.

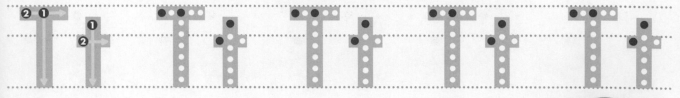

Tt Tt Tt Tt Tt Tt Tt Tt Tt

Tom tasted a tart.

Draw lines from the **t** to the words that have a **t** in them.

turtle

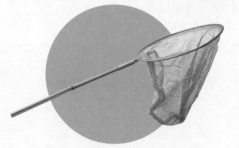

net

letter

coin

boat

20

Trace the uppercase and lowercase **u**'s.

Uu Uu Uu Uu

Una looked up.

Write the **u**'s in these words.

n_____ts

p_____ppy

j_____mp

m_____g

dr_____m

pl_____m

Trace the uppercase and lowercase **v**'s.

V v V V V v V V V v V V

Vince is a vet.

Check the words that start with **v**.

☐ **pan**

☐ **van**

☐ **violin**

☐ **snake**

☐ **vase**

☐ **map**

Trace the uppercase and lowercase **w**'s.

W w W w W w

Willa wears a watch.

Find and circle six **w**'s.

m m v
v w v
w m v m
w w v
v v m
m m w

Trace the uppercase and lowercase **x**'s.

Xx Xx Xx Xx Xx

Max saw an ox.

Write the **x**'s in these words.

 bo___

 fo___

 e___it

Trace the uppercase and lowercase **y**'s.

Yy Yy Yy Yy Yy

Yasmin loves yogurt.

Draw lines from the **y** to the words that have a **y** in them.

 yo-yo

y

bear

fly

 yak

Trace the uppercase and lowercase z's.

Zz Zz Zz Zz Zz

Zack made a pizza.

Follow the **z**'s to help the **z**ebra find the **z**oo.

Start →

z	z	z	y	x
w	y	x	z	x	w
x	y	z	z	z	z	y	x
w	w	z	x	w	x	y	w
y	x	z	x	w	w
x	w	z	z	y	x
y	y	w	x	z	z

→ Finish

ZOO

Things that go

Color it. Trace it. Write it.

 car | car |

 bus | bus |

 boat | boat |

 bike | bike |

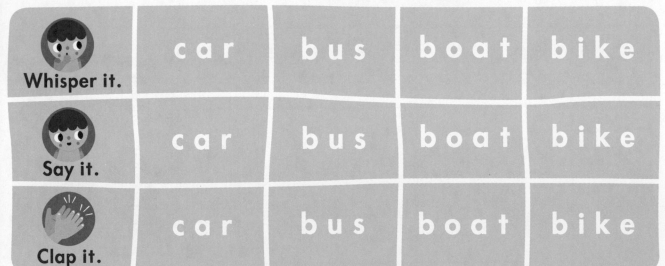

Whisper it. car bus boat bike

Say it. car bus boat bike

Clap it. car bus boat bike

Which word?

Write the words.

This is a **bike** ....

This is a ....

This is a ....

This is a ....

Unscramble the letters and write the words.
Put the correct sticker by each word.

s u b **bus** ....

r a c ....

a b o t ....

k e b i ....

Things to do

Color it. Trace it. Write it.

run	run	

jump	jump	

play	play	

sleep	sleep	

	run	jump	play	sleep
Whisper it.	run	jump	play	sleep
Say it.	run	jump	play	sleep
Clap it.	run	jump	play	sleep

Word match

Match the words to the pictures.

sleep   **jump**

run   **play**

Write a spelling word below each picture.

play ....

....

Animals

Color it. Trace it. Write it.

 cat | cat |

 dog | dog |

 bee | bee |

 bird | bird |

Whisper it.	c a t	d o g	b e e	b i r d
Say it.	c a t	d o g	b e e	b i r d
Clap it.	c a t	d o g	b e e	b i r d

Label it!

Finish the sentences in the speech bubbles.

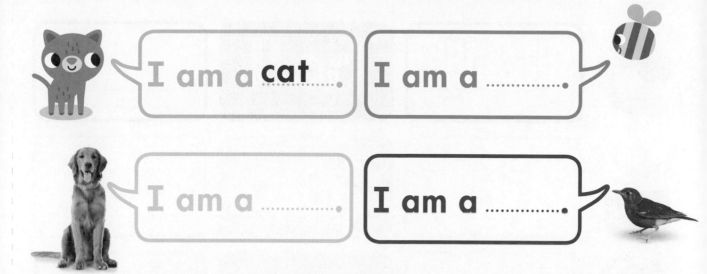

Sticker the labels below the pictures.

Playtime

Color it. Trace it. Write it.

ball | ball |

drum | drum |

toy | toy |

book | book |

 **Whisper it.**	ball	drum	toy	book
Say it.	ball	drum	toy	book
Clap it.	ball	drum	toy	book

Find the letters

Circle the letters to spell the words.

 i (b) w (a) v p (l) x g (l)

 t v b o r j s y u a

 m b w o r o k e t

drum s d h r l q u z m

Circle the rhyming words. Use the picture clues to help.

toy   top   (boy)   day

ball   bat   wall   bell

book   boot   kick   look   

drum   fall   dog   thumb

Opposites

Color it.　Trace it.　Write it.

  go | go |

 stop | stop |

 big | big |

 little | little |

Whisper it.	go	stop	big	little
Say it.	go	stop	big	little
Clap it.	go	stop	big	little

Which word?

Write the words.

The ball is ....

This means ....

The ball is ....

This means ....

Unscramble the letters and write the words.
Put the correct sticker by each word.

g i b ....

o g ....

t e t i l l ....

p o s t ....

More opposites

Color it. Trace it. Write it.

 good good

 bad bad

 happy happy

 sad sad

	good	bad	happy	sad
Whisper it.	good	bad	happy	sad
Say it.	good	bad	happy	sad
Clap it.	good	bad	happy	sad

Word search

Find the words in the word search.

good	bad	happy	sad

y	**g**	**o**	**o**	**d**	c	h
i	b	v	a	g	k	p
o	d	j	m	h	o	b
r	e	o	s	a	t	a
y	a	k	k	p	m	d
s	a	d	x	p	e	l
o	l	y	m	y	d	j

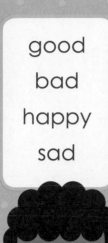

Draw lines to match the words to their opposites.

good	sad
happy	bad
sad	happy
bad	good

Where is it?

Color it. Trace it. Write it.

| up | up | |

| down | down | |

| over | over | |

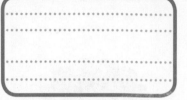

| under | under | |

	up	down	over	under
Whisper it.	up	down	over	under
Say it.	up	down	over	under
Clap it.	up	down	over	under

Word match

Match the words to the pictures.

up   down

over   under

Write a spelling word below each picture.

....

....

People

Color it. Trace it. Write it.

 boy | **boy** |

 girl | girl |

 man | **man** |

 woman | woman |

	boy	girl	man	woman
Whisper it.	boy	girl	man	woman
Say it.	boy	girl	man	woman
Clap it.	boy	girl	man	woman

Label it!

Finish the sentences in the speech bubbles.

I am a ....　　I am a ....

I am a ....　　I am a ....

Sticker the labels below the pictures.

Family

Color it. Trace it. Write it.

 sister | sister |
 brother | brother |
 mother | mother |
 father | father |

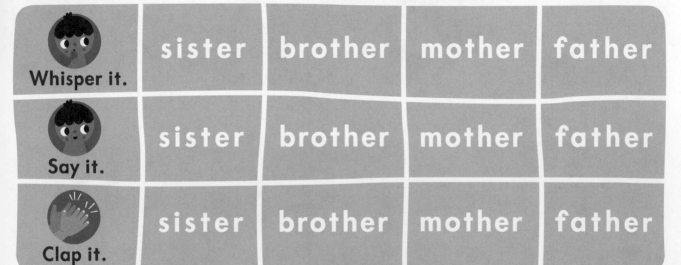

Whisper it.	sister	brother	mother	father
Say it.	sister	brother	mother	father
Clap it.	sister	brother	mother	father

Word search

Find the words in the word search.

sister
brother
mother
father

a	w	y	y	e	c	d	p	s
k	n	s	t	o	b	i	f	i
r	i	m	l	j	q	t	k	s
b	r	o	t	h	e	r	e	t
s	u	t	d	l	y	h	q	e
m	y	h	b	s	m	v	r
q	j	e	p	y	g	p	l	w
s	v	r	z	a	k	o	g	n
f	u	h	f	a	t	h	e	r

Match the words to the pictures.

father

sister

mother

brother

The rainbow

Finish coloring each word the correct color.

yellow

purple

brown

red

blue

green

orange

black

Now trace each word with the correct colored pencil.

red

green

orange

brown

blue

yellow

black

purple

Label it!

Sticker the correct color labels on the rainbow.

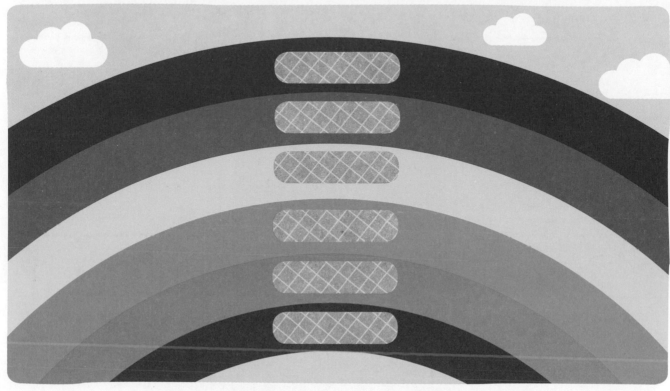

Finish the sentences.

This top is ....

This top is ....

This top is ....

This top is ....

Sight words 1

Color it. Trace it. Write it.

me	me	
we	we	
he	he	
she	she	

Here **we** are.

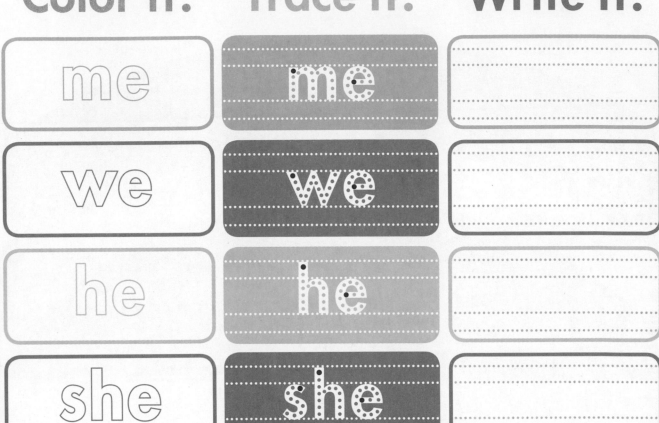

Whisper it.	me	we	he	she
Say it.	me	we	he	she
Clap it.	me	we	he	she

# Word art

Use the key to finish coloring the picture.

me = orange   we = blue   he = green   she = red

Sight words 2

Color it.   Trace it.   Write it.

Color it.	Trace it.	Write it.
no	no	
yes	yes	
to	to	
like	like	

He said **yes**.

She said **no**.

Whisper it.	no	yes	to	like
Say it.	no	yes	to	like
Clap it.	no	yes	to	like

Word maze

Follow the word **like** to help the rabbits reach the carrots.

Sight words ③

Color it.   Trace it.   Write it.

Color it.	Trace it.	Write it.
and	and	
for	for	
but	but	
with	with	

This is **for** you.

	and	for	but	with
Whisper it.	and	for	but	with
Say it.	and	for	but	with
Clap it.	and	for	but	with

Find the word

Circle the word that is spelled correctly in each row.

dna (and) nad dan

rof orf for rfor

but bot bul ubt

wiht witt whit with

Sight words 4

Color it.   Trace it.   Write it.

so	so	
can	can	
now	now	
said	said	

I **can** do it **now**.

	so	can	now	said
Whisper it.	so	can	now	said
Say it.	so	can	now	said
Clap it.	so	can	now	said

Count the words

Help Pippa count the words. Write the numbers in the boxes.
Circle the word that appears most often.

so [8]   **can** [ ]   now [ ]   said [ ]

so can **can** now
now
SO can so **NOW**
NOW so said **SO**
said **can** so
now now now
said now
SO so **NOW**
now now
can said

Sight words 5

Color it.　　Trace it.　　Write it.

do	do	
has	has	
had	had	
have	have	

She **has** a balloon.

Whisper it.	do	has	had	have
Say it.	do	has	had	have
Clap it.	do	has	had	have

Word search

Help Harry find each sight word in the word search.

do ✓   has ✓   had ✓   have ✓

```
a  d  e  m  a  i  g  e  p
h  o  e  h  a  d  a  o  a
m  e  u  s  h  e  d  r  h
h  u  e  a  u  h  a  s  a
a  a  v  e  d  a  o  e  e
v  m  v  a  e  s
e  s  a  i  b  a
a  v  o  s  d  v
```

Sight words 6

Color it.　Trace it.　Write it.

the	the	
they	they	
this	this	
that	that	

They like **this** dog.

Whisper it.	the	they	this	that
Say it.	the	they	this	that
Clap it.	the	they	this	that

56

Link the letters

Help Eve find and link the letters to spell the words.

the **they** **this** **that**

i h u t t h e t j

t t h a t a h

t a b

h e y h

a x i

t h i s

h t t

w o m

Sight words

Color it.   Trace it.   Write it.

Color it.	Trace it.	Write it.
why	why	
who	who	
what	what	
when	when	

Who is that?

Whisper it.	why	who	what	when
Say it.	why	who	what	when
Clap it.	why	who	what	when

Word art

Use the key to finish coloring the picture.

why = yellow   who = purple   what = blue   when = red

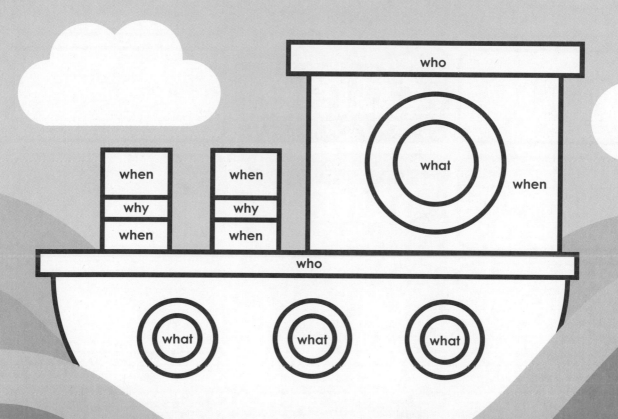

Sight words 8

Color it. Trace it. Write it.

come	come	
came	came	
some	some	
same	same	

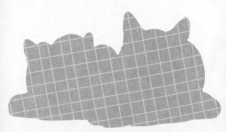

Some cats look the **same**.

Whisper it.	come	came	some	same
Say it.	come	came	some	same
Clap it.	come	came	some	same

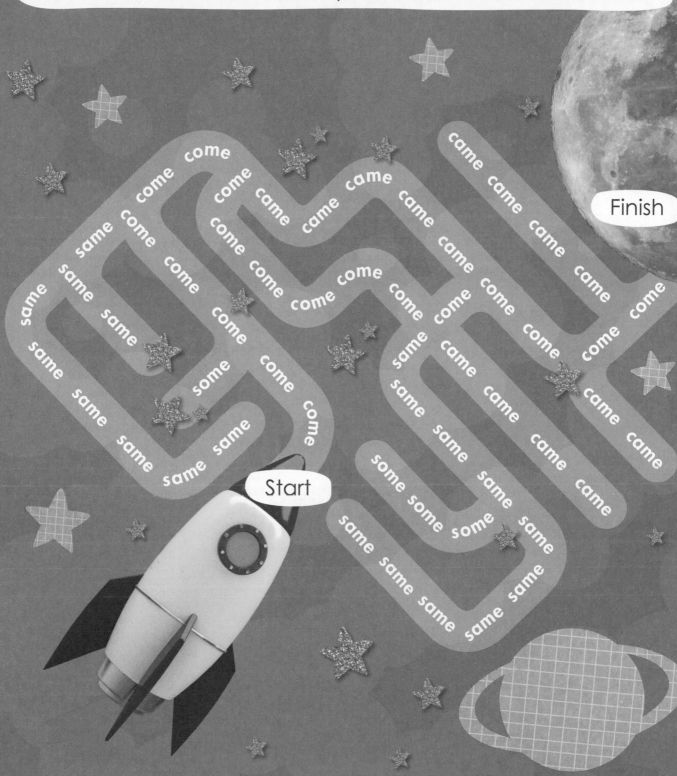

Word maze

Follow the word **come** to help the rocket reach the moon.

Finish

Start

Sight words 9

Color it.　Trace it.　Write it.

Color	Trace	Write
went	went	
away	away	
from	from	
here	here	

She **went away from here.**

	went	away	from	here
Whisper it.	went	away	from	here
Say it.	went	away	from	here
Clap it.	went	away	from	here

Find the word

Circle the word that is spelled correctly in each row.

wint wont whent **went**

ayaw awey **away** awya

from fram fron form

heer nere hare **here**

Sight words ⑩

Color it.   Trace it.   Write it.

Color it.	Trace it.	Write it.
make	make	
take	take	
where	where	
there	there	

I **make** cupcakes.

Whisper it.	make	take	where	there
Say it.	make	take	where	there
Clap it.	make	take	where	there

Count the words

Help Tom count the words. Write the numbers in the boxes.
Circle the word that appears most often.

make ☐ **take** ☐ **where** ☐ **there** ☐

make where make
make take make
there make there
make make
make take
there there
where take
there make
make where
take where

The **wh** sound

Say the words. Circle **wh** in each word.

wheel

whistle

whale

wheat

Read the question words aloud.
Circle the one that doesn't start with **wh**.

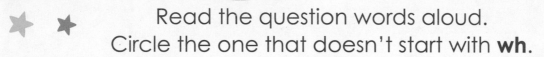

when   why

when   what

how   which

The **wr** sound

Say the words. Circle **wr** in each word.

wrench

wrap

write

wrong

Say each word and write **wr**.

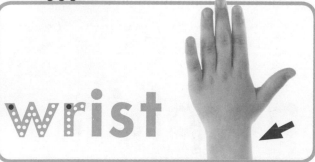
wrist

wring

wreck

wren

ph and gh

Say the words. Circle **ph** in **pink** and **gh** in **blue**.

phone

rough

photo

tough

Say each word and trace **ph** or **gh**.

laugh

dolphin

trophy

cough

gn and kn

Say the words. Circle **gn** in **red** and **kn** in **purple**.

gnome

knight

sign

knife

Say each word and trace **gn** or **kn**.

gnaw

knit

knob

gnu

ch and tch

Say the words. Circle **ch** in **blue** and **tch** in **red**.

catch

march

peach

watch

★ ★ Say each word and trace **ch** or **tch**.

hatch

lunch

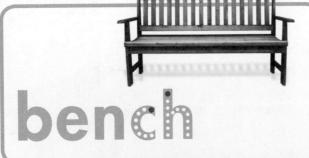
bench

match

ng and nk

Say the words. Circle **ng** in **orange** and **nk** in **pink**.

king

pink

drink

gong

Say each word and trace **ng** or **nk**.

wing

wink

hang

bunk

sh and th

Say the words. Circle **sh** in **blue** and **th** in **red**.

thumb

ship

fish

teeth

Say each word and trace **sh** or **th**.

brush

three

moth

sheep

72

br and bl

Say the words. Circle **br** in **orange** and **bl** in **green**.

bread

blocks

blanket

branch

Say each word and trace **br** or **bl**.

blink

bridge

blue

broom

Silent e

A **silent e** makes the other vowel say its name.
The other vowel goes from **short** to **long**.
Say the words and trace the vowels.

man | mane

pet | Pete

pin | pine

hop | hope

cub | cube

Silent e practice

Circle the correct word.

tap
(tape)

rat
rate

hat
hate

kit
kite

con
cone

rid
ride

glob
globe

hug
huge

cut
cute

tub
tube

Bossy r words

When **r** comes after a vowel, the vowel sound changes.
Circle the words with **ar** in them in **blue**.
Circle the words with **or** in them in **red**.
Then draw lines to match each word to its picture.

car

fork

barn

horn

harp

corn

shark

horse

star

storm

More bossy r words

Say the words. Trace the **er** sound in each word.
It is spelled three ways here.

surf girl

fern turkey

water bird

nurse baker

Write two other ways **er** is spelled here.

 er

The oy sound

Say the words. Trace the **oy** sound in each word.
It is spelled two ways here.

coin

boy

joy

noisy

Circle the letters that make the **oy** sound.

point

annoy

toy

toilet

The long a sound

Say the words. Trace the **long a** sound in each word. It is spelled three ways here.

 cake sail

hay mail

train gate

wave tray

Write two other ways **long a** is spelled here.

a-e

The long e sound

Say the words. Trace the **long e** sound in each word.
It is spelled four ways here.

bee

alien

puppy

peas

Circle the letters that make the **long e** sound.

cheese

shield

twenty 20

seal

The long i sound

Say the words. Trace the **long i** sound in each word.
It is spelled four ways here.

pie

fly

cry

tie

bike

spy

tights

knight

Write three other ways **long i** is spelled here.

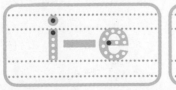
i–e

The long o sound

Say the words. Trace the **long o** sound in each word.
It is spelled two ways here.

b**oa**t

r**ow**

yell**ow**

s**oa**p

Circle the letters that make the **long o** sound.

coat

bow

mow

toast

The **ow** sound

Say the words. Trace the **ow** sound in each word.
It is spelled two ways here.

 house  cow

 howl mouse

 crown cloud

owl shout

Write two ways the **ow** sound is spelled here.

The long oo sound

Say the words. Trace the **long oo** sound in each word.
It is spelled four ways here.

moose

blue

tube

chew

 Circle the letters that make the **long oo** sound.

goose

glue

rude

stew

Long oo and short oo

Say **zoo**. Circle the words with this **long oo** sound in **purple**.
Say **book**. Circle the words with this **short oo** sound in green.
Then draw lines to match each word to its picture.

Woof!

woof

moon

wood

igloo

cookie

boots

foot

spoon

hook

balloon

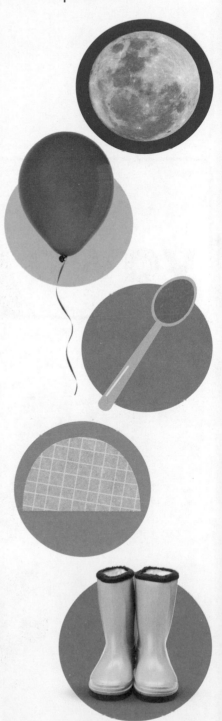

The aw sound

Say the words. Trace the **aw** sound in each word.
It is spelled two ways here.

saw

ball

yawn

wall

Circle the letters that make the **aw** sound.

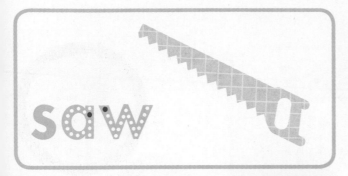

draw

fall

paw

walk

The air sound

Say the words. Trace the **air** sound in each word.
It is spelled three ways here.

pair

hare

bear

square

Circle the letters that make the **air** sound.

chair

share

pear

tear

Start with a capital letter

Circle the capital letters.

(C) v S b P

r F t A o

Sentences always start with a capital letter.
Trace the capital letters in these sentences.

It was hot.

We had ice cream.

She took a swim.

He took a swim, too.

Ending sentences

Most sentences end with a period. This is a small dot.
Trace and write some periods on the line.

Circle the periods in these sentences.

We like to cook.

We make a mess.

Add periods to these sentences.

We like to read

I like to skate

Capital letters

Names start with a capital letter. Circle the correct names.

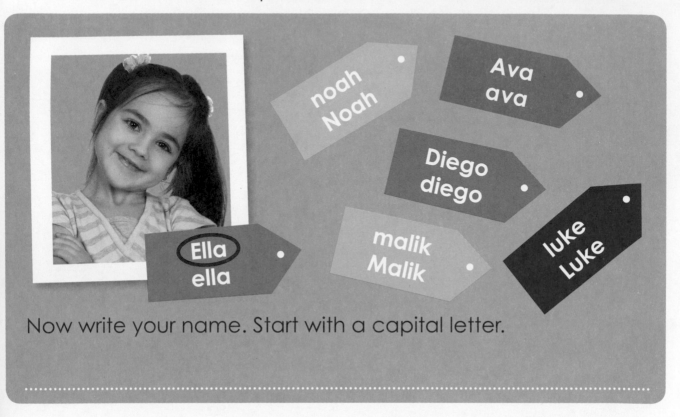

noah
Noah

Ava
ava

Diego
diego

Ella
ella

malik
Malik

luke
Luke

Now write your name. Start with a capital letter.

Names of places have capital letters, too.
Trace the capital letters.

London   New York

Exclamation marks

Trace and write some exclamation marks.

! ! ! ! ! ! !

Add exclamation marks to the speech bubbles.

Question marks

At the end of a question, write a question mark.
Trace and write some question marks.

? ? ? ? ? ?

Add a question mark to each question.

Hi! What is your name

Why is the cat in the box

Who made this mess

Where is the bathroom

Be the teacher

Help Jack fix the mistakes in his writing.
Write what should be there.

Hi   my name is jack

i go to school

this is my classroom

do you like it

Speech bubbles

What are the people in these pictures saying?
Write some words in the speech bubbles.

Gift list

Pretend it's your birthday. Write 4 of these things on your wish list. Then write 2 more things you would like.

truck

bike

puppy

dinosaur

Birthday list

....

....

....

....

....

....

book

game

crayons

ball

doll

building bricks

clothes

Doing words

Doing words tell people about actions.
Trace the doing words in these sentences.

They ride.

He crawls.

We jump.

It flies.

She sleeps.

You clap.

Describing words

Describing words tell people what things are like.
Circle the correct describing word for each picture.

(**happy**)   sad

huge   tiny

sweet   stinky

curly   straight

red   blue

old   new

boring   scary

fluffy   bald

Write sentences

Write a sentence about each picture. Start each sentence with a capital letter. Finish it with a period.

....

....

 Now draw a picture and write a sentence about it.

Write one or two sentences about the picture.
Use capital letters and periods.

....

....

....

....

....

....

Draw a picture of you doing something you like.
Write a sentence about it. Use capital letters and periods.

....

....

Write a poem

Read the poem about a cat. Write a poem about another animal.
Use doing words and describing words.

Our Cat
Fluffy
Purry
Long tail
Running and jumping
So cute!

....

....

....

....

....

....

My best friend

Answer the questions. Write in sentences.

Who is your best friend?

My best friend is

....

....

What do you like about this person?

....

....

What does this person look like?

....

....

....

Draw a picture of your best friend.

Write one other thing about this person.

....

....

How to build a house

How do you make a house with building bricks?
Write about how to do it.

To build a house, you will need

....

Instructions

1 **First,** make the walls.

....

2 **Then,** ....

....

3 **Finally,** ....

....

Draw a picture of the house you would build.

What do you think?

Which is better: a soft toy or a toy truck?
Write what you think.

toy truck

soft toy

I think a .... is better than a ....

because ....

....

Also, ...

....

Draw a picture of a soft toy or toy truck you would like.

Dinosaur adventure

Look at the pictures. Draw a picture to show what happens next.
Make up names and write the story beside the pictures.

Tell the story

Look at the picture and make up your own story.

My story's title is:

....

It is about a child called ....

One day, ...

....

....

But then, ...

....

In the end, ...

....

Draw another picture to go with the story.

Trace the letters with your finger.

apple

anchor

Trace the **a**'s.

A A A A A A A A

a a a a a a a a a

Trace and write more **a**'s.

A A A

a a a

Trace the sentence.

Andy the alligator

ate apples.

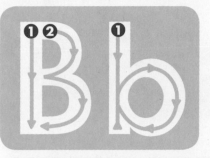

butterfly

ball

Trace the **b**'s.

B B B B B B B B B

b b b b b b b b b

Trace and write more **b**'s.

B B B

b b b

Trace the sentence.

Bella the bear
bakes bread.

C c

cat

car

Trace the **c**'s.

C C C C C C C C

c c c c c c c c c

Trace and write more **c**'s.

C C C

c c c

Trace the sentence.

Carla the cow
likes cupcakes.

doll **d**og

Trace the **d**'s.

D D D D D D D D

Trace and write more **d**'s.

D D D

Trace the sentence.

Dylan the dinosaur danced at the disco.

exercise

elephant

Trace the **e**'s.

E E E E E E E E E E

e e e e e e e e e e

Trace and write more **e**'s.

E E E

e e e

Trace the sentence.

Ellie the eagle

eats eggs.

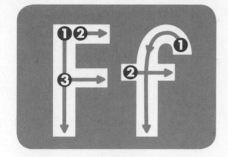

Trace and write **f**'s.

F F F f f f

F F f f

Trace the sentence.

Fay the fish has
five green fins.

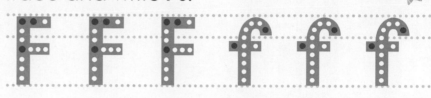

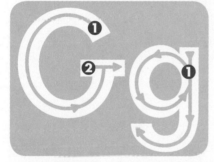

Trace and write **g**'s.

G G G g g g

G G g g

Trace the sentence.

Greg the gorilla
gave a growl.

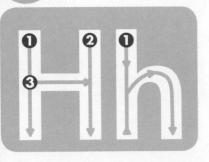

horse

house

Trace the **h**'s.

H H H H H H H H H H

h h h h h h h h h h

Trace and write more **h**'s.

H H H

h h h

Trace the sentence.

Holly is a hairy
hamster.

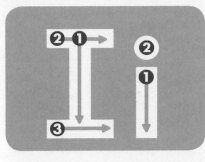

iguana

ink

Trace the **i**'s.

Trace and write more **i**'s.

Trace the sentence.

Isaac the

insect is ill.

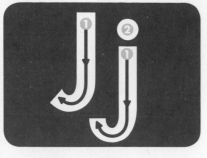

Trace and write **j**'s.

J J J j j j

J J j j

Trace the sentence.

Jenny the jaguar is in the jungle.

Trace and write **k**'s.

K K K k k k

K K k k

Trace the sentence.

Kyle the kitten is kind.

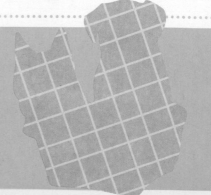

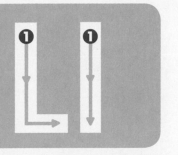

lamp

lion

Trace the **l**'s.

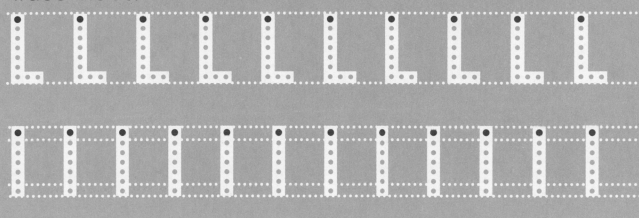

Trace and write more **l**'s.

Trace the sentence.

Lily the lizard
loves lunch.

mug

monkey

Trace the **m**'s.

M M M M M M M

m m m m m m m

Trace and write more **m**'s.

M M M

m m m

Trace the sentence.

Matt the mouse
drinks milk.

nurse

necklace

Trace the **n**'s.

N N N N N N N N

n n n n n n n n

Trace and write more **n**'s.

N N N

n n n

Trace the sentence.

Nicola the newt

needs a nap.

zzz

117

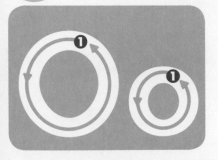

octag**o**n

ostrich

Trace the o's.

Trace and write more o's.

Trace the sentence.

Ollie the otter
buys oranges.

parrot **p**iano

Trace the **p**'s.

P P P P P P P

p p p p p p p

Trace and write more **p**'s.

P P P

p p p

Trace the sentence.

Poppy the panda
paints pretty pictures.

Trace and write **q**'s.

Q Q Q Q q q q

Q Q q q

Trace the sentence.

Quincy is a
quiet quail.

Trace and write **r**'s.

R R R R r r r

R R r r

Trace the sentence.

Ruby the rabbit
runs in the rain.

snake   **s**andcastle

Trace the **s**'s.

Trace and write more **s**'s.

Trace the sentence.

Sam the spider spins a web.

121

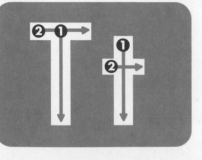

train

tiger

Trace the t's.

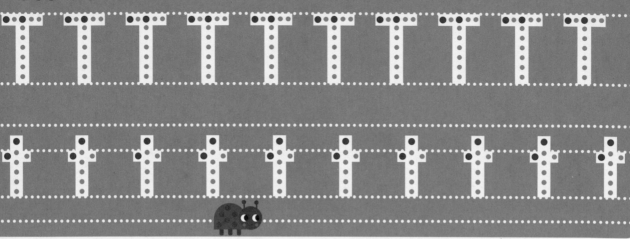

Trace and write more t's.

Trace the sentence.

Tara the tortoise
ate two tomatoes.

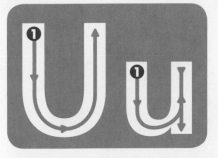

umbrella **u**mpire

Trace the **u**'s.

U U U U U U U U

u u u u u u u u u u

Trace and write more **u**'s.

U U U

u u u

Trace the sentence.

Ursula the urchin
lives underwater.

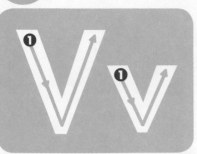

vase

volcano

Trace the **v**'s.

Trace and write more **v**'s.

Trace the sentence.

Vinnie the vulture

lives in a cave.

wand **w**atermelon

Trace the **w**'s.

W W W W W W

W W W W W W

W W W

W W W

Trace the sentence.

Willow is a

wise walrus.

Trace and write **x**'s.

X X X X x x x

X X x x

Trace the sentence.

Xander the fox
met an ox.

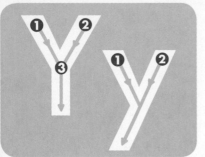

Trace and write **y**'s.

Y Y Y Y y y y

Y Y y y

Trace the sentence.

Yasmin the
yak is yellow.

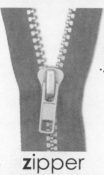

Z z

zipper

zoo

Trace the **z**'s.

ZZZZZZZZ

zzzzzzzz

Trace and write more **z**'s.

Z Z Z

Z Z Z

Trace the sentence.

Zack is a
lazy zebra.

What's the same?

Circle the picture that is the same as the first one.

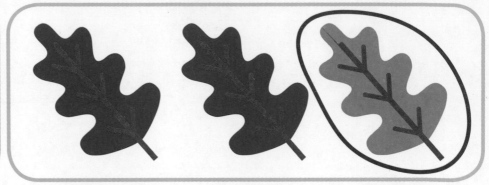

What's different?

Circle the picture that is different.

Match the amounts

Draw lines to match the groups with the same number of items.

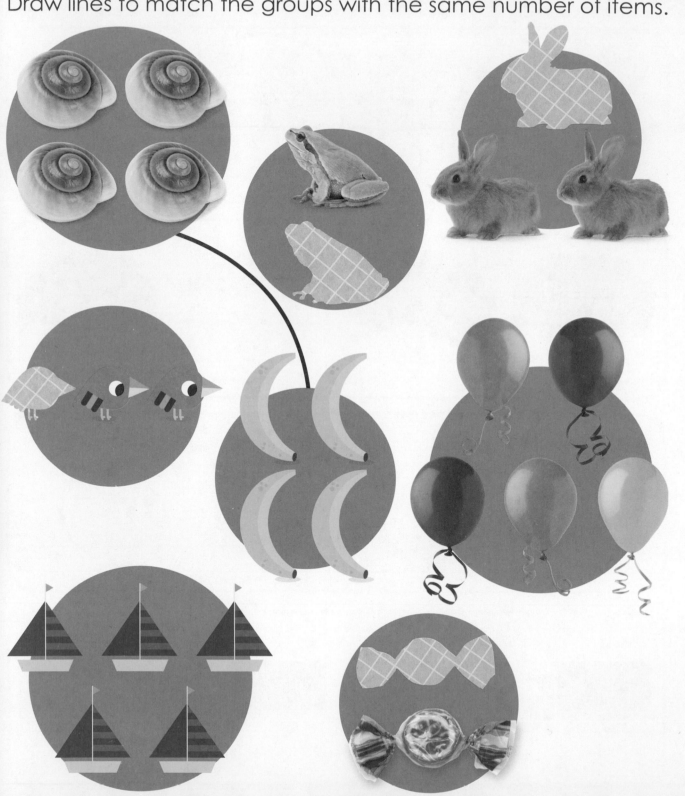

Up and down

Write the words under the arrows.

down

up

Color the arrows that point up **blue**.
Color the arrows that point down **red**.

Left and right

Trace the words under the hands.

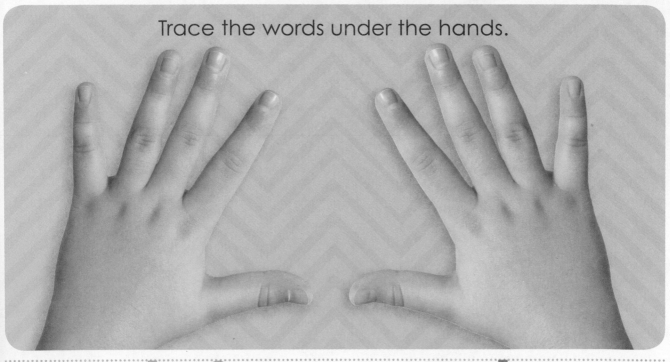

 left right

Draw lines to match the arrows with the correct directions.

Left and right

Sticker the **right** sock next to the **left** sock.
Sticker the **left** shoe next to the **right** shoe.

Draw a person to the **left** of the tree.
Draw a house to the **right** of the tree.

Name the groups

Look at the pictures. Circle the correct group name.

cats (birds) fish

boots books food

hats food mice

trees cars cats

balls dolls toys

Find the groups

Circle the members of the group.

cats

fruit

beetles

flowers

planes

Two-way sorting

Draw different lines to sort the animals.

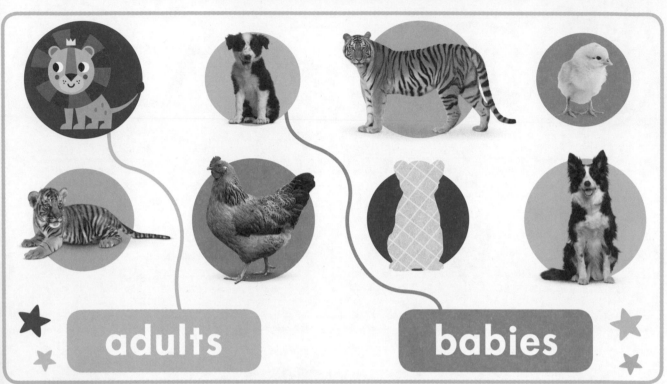

adults

babies

big cats

dogs

birds

Three-way sorting

Draw different lines to sort the buttons.

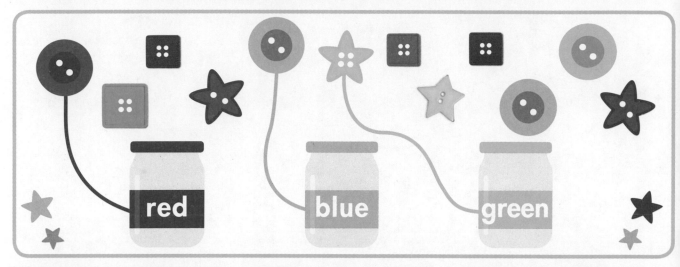

red   blue   green

round ○   square □   star ☆

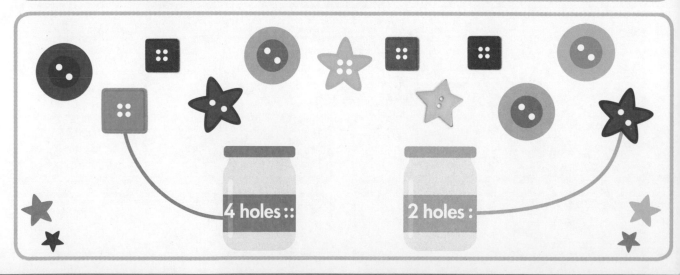

4 holes ::   2 holes :

Get ready for graphs

Write the number of each group in the picture.

1

Make a graph

Count the sea creatures.
Color one box for each group member.

starfish	sharks	seahorses	fish	crabs
5				
4				
3				
2				
1				

Circle the group that appears most often.

Which came first?

Write a **1** in the box by the thing that happened first.
Write a **2** in the box by the thing that happened later.

1

2

Order the pictures

Write **1**, **2**, or **3** in each box to show the order.

2

1

3

True or false

Circle **true** for the things that are in the picture.
Circle **false** for the things that are not in the picture.

The children are in a castle.	true	(false)
The children are all boys.	true	false
They are in a classroom.	true	false
There are pictures on the wall.	true	false
There is a dog in the room.	true	false

Fact or fantasy

Write **R** for **real** by the things that could happen.
Write **P** for **pretend** by the things that are make believe.

............**R**............

....

....

....

....

....

Hansel and Gretel

Use your number stickers to put the pictures in order from **1** to **4**.

They found a candy house.

Then the witch made them work hard.

They locked up the witch and ran home.

Hansel and Gretel were lost.

Cinderella

Write the numbers **1** to **6** in order.

Sticker and color the last picture, and then tell the story.

⑦ happily ever after

One to five

Trace the numbers and words. Then count the objects.

1 one

fox

2 two

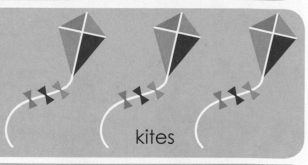
trucks

3 three

kites

4 four

Popsicles

5 five

hippos

Six to ten

Trace the numbers and words. Then color the objects.

 **six**

pigs

 **seven**

planes

 **eight**
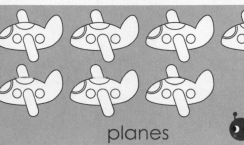
caps

nine
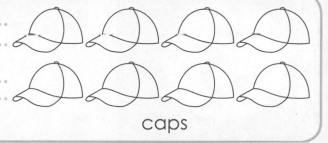
crayons

 **ten**

monsters

Match the numbers

Draw lines to match the numbers with the groups.

1
2
3
4
5

Match the numbers

Draw lines to match the numbers with the groups.

Eleven to fifteen

Trace the numbers and words. Then count the objects.

11 eleven

starfish

12 twelve

sharks

13 thirteen

fish

14 fourteen

buckets

15 fifteen

shovels

Sixteen to twenty

Trace the numbers and words. Then count the objects.

16 sixteen

ants

17 seventeen

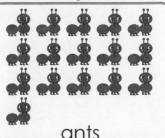
flies

18 eighteen

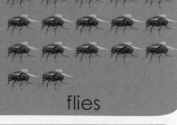
bugs

19 nineteen

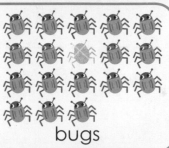
butterflies

20 twenty

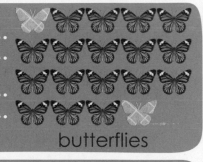
snails

Ten and ones

Start with ten and add some ones.

Ten ladybugs and one more ladybug makes **11** ladybugs.

10 + 1 = (11)

Ten cars and two more cars makes ...... cars.

10 + 2 = ◯

Ten flowers and three more flowers makes ...... flowers.

10 + 3 = ◯

Ten apples and four more apples makes ...... apples.

10 + 4 = ◯

Ten dinosaurs and five more dinosaurs makes ...... dinosaurs.

10 + 5 = ◯

Ten cats and six more cats makes ...... cats.

10 + 6 = ◯

Ten leaves and seven more leaves makes ...... leaves.

10 + 7 = ◯

Ten hats and eight more hats makes ...... hats.

10 + 8 = ◯

Ten mice and nine more mice makes ...... mice.

10 + 9 = ◯

Ten balls and ten more balls makes ...... balls.

10 + 10 = ◯

Hundreds charts

Finish shading all the numbers with **3** in them **green**.

Shade all the numbers with **5** in them **red**.

Shade all the numbers with **7** in them **blue**.

Shade all the numbers with **9** in them **yellow**.

1	2	3	4	5	6	7	8	9	10
11	12	13	14	15	16	17	18	19	20
21	22	23	24	25	26	27	28	29	30
31	32	33	34	35	36	37	38	39	40
41	42	43	44	45	46	47	48	49	50
51	52	53	54	55	56	57	58	59	60
61	62	63	64	65	66	67	68	69	70
71	72	73	74	75	76	77	78	79	80
81	82	83	84	85	86	87	88	89	90
91	92	93	94	95	96	97	98	99	100

Shade all the numbers with **2** in them **orange**.

Shade all the numbers with **4** in them **pink**.

Shade all the numbers with **6** in them **purple**.

Shade all the numbers with **8** in them **brown**.

1	2	3	4	5	6	7	8	9	10
11	12	13	14	15	16	17	18	19	20
21	22	23	24	25	26	27	28	29	30
31	32	33	34	35	36	37	38	39	40
41	42	43	44	45	46	47	48	49	50
51	52	53	54	55	56	57	58	59	60
61	62	63	64	65	66	67	68	69	70
71	72	73	74	75	76	77	78	79	80
81	82	83	84	85	86	87	88	89	90
91	92	93	94	95	96	97	98	99	100

Hundreds charts

Fill in the missing numbers.

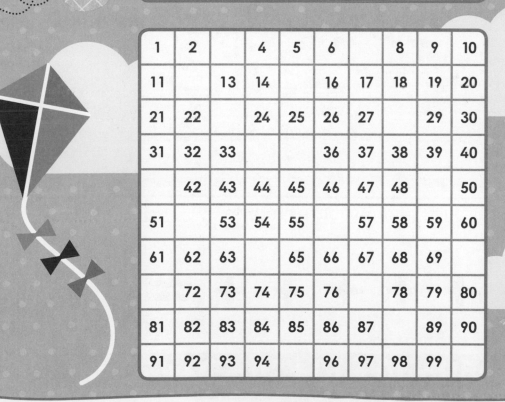

1	2	3	4		6	7	8	9	10
11	12	13	14	15	16	17		19	20
21		23	24	25	26	27	28	29	30
31	32		34	35	36	37	38	39	40
41	42	43	44	45	46	47	48	49	
51	52	53	54	55	56		58	59	60
61	62	63	64	65	66	67	68		70
71	72	73		75	76	77	78	79	80
81	82	83	84	85		87	88	89	90
	92	93	94	95	96	97	98	99	100

1	2		4	5	6		8	9	10
11		13	14		16	17	18	19	20
21	22		24	25	26	27		29	30
31	32	33			36	37	38	39	40
	42	43	44	45	46	47	48		50
51		53	54	55		57	58	59	60
61	62	63		65	66	67	68	69	
	72	73	74	75	76		78	79	80
81	82	83	84	85	86	87		89	90
91	92	93	94		96	97	98	99	

Counting by tens

Count the groups of ten.

Three groups of ten stars makes **30** stars.

$$10 + 10 + 10 = 30$$

Four groups of ten hearts makes .... hearts.

$$10 + 10 + 10 + 10 = \bigcirc$$

Six groups of ten circles makes .... circles.

$$10 + 10 + 10 + 10 + 10 + 10 = \bigcirc$$

Eight groups of ten squares makes .... squares.

$$10 + 10 + 10 + 10 + 10 + 10 + 10 + 10 = \bigcirc$$

 # Tens and ones

Count the groups of ten and add the ones.

Three groups of ten stars and **two** stars makes **32** stars.

★★★★★ + ★★★★★ + ★★★★★ + ★ = ★★★★★★★★★★...

10 + 10 + 10 + 2 = ◯

Three groups of ten hearts and **three** hearts makes .... hearts.

10 + 10 + 10 + 3 = ◯

Five groups of ten circles and **three** circles makes .... circles.

10 + 10 + 10 + 10 + 10 + 3 = ◯

Five groups of ten squares and **four** squares makes .... squares.

10 + 10 + 10 + 10 + 10 + 4 = ◯

More or fewer

For each pair, circle the group with **more** in it.

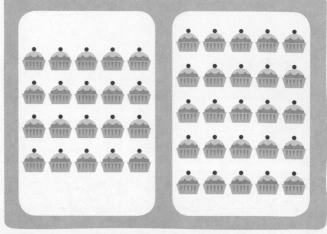

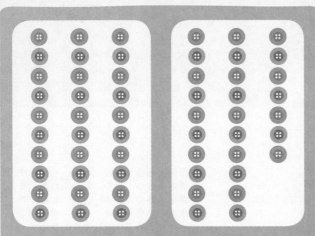

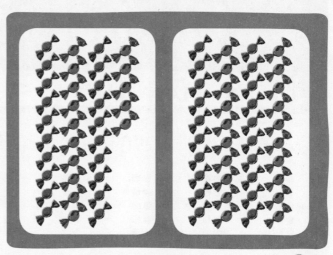

For each pair, circle the group with **fewer** in it.

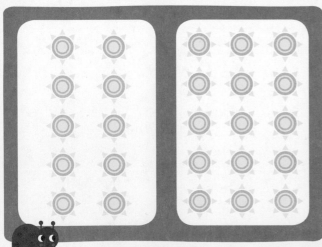

Skip counting by 2's

Finish counting the shoes. Count by **2**'s.

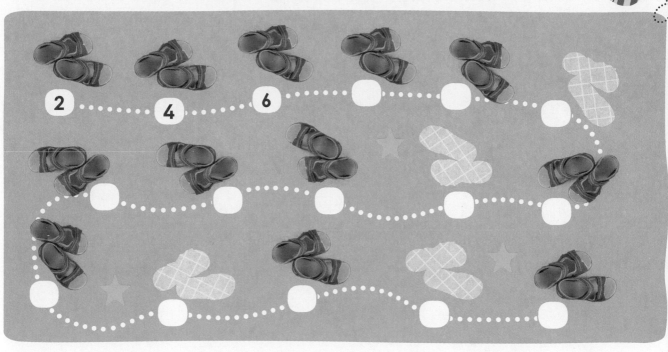

Use an **orange** pencil to finish skip counting by **2**'s up to 100.

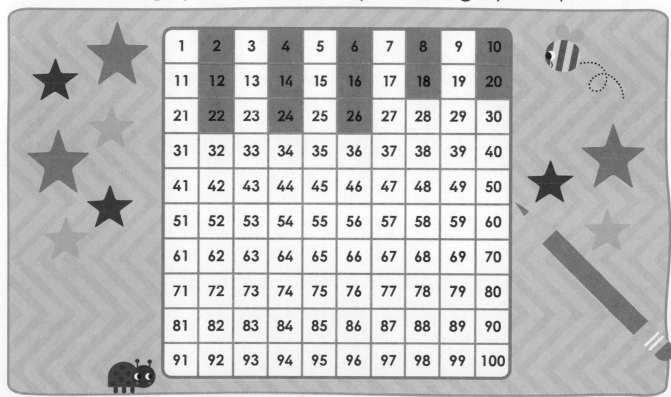

1	2	3	4	5	6	7	8	9	10
11	12	13	14	15	16	17	18	19	20
21	22	23	24	25	26	27	28	29	30
31	32	33	34	35	36	37	38	39	40
41	42	43	44	45	46	47	48	49	50
51	52	53	54	55	56	57	58	59	60
61	62	63	64	65	66	67	68	69	70
71	72	73	74	75	76	77	78	79	80
81	82	83	84	85	86	87	88	89	90
91	92	93	94	95	96	97	98	99	100

Skip counting by 5's

Finish counting the fingers. Count by **5**'s.

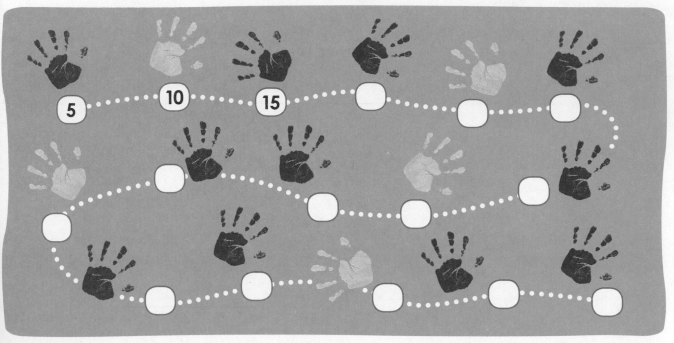

5 · 10 · 15 · · · · ·

Use a **green** pencil to finish skip counting by **5**'s up to 100.

1	2	3	4	5	6	7	8	9	10
11	12	13	14	15	16	17	18	19	20
21	22	23	24	25	26	27	28	29	30
31	32	33	34	35	36	37	38	39	40
41	42	43	44	45	46	47	48	49	50
51	52	53	54	55	56	57	58	59	60
61	62	63	64	65	66	67	68	69	70
71	72	73	74	75	76	77	78	79	80
81	82	83	84	85	86	87	88	89	90
91	92	93	94	95	96	97	98	99	100

Skip counting by 10's

Finish counting the toes. Count by **10**'s.

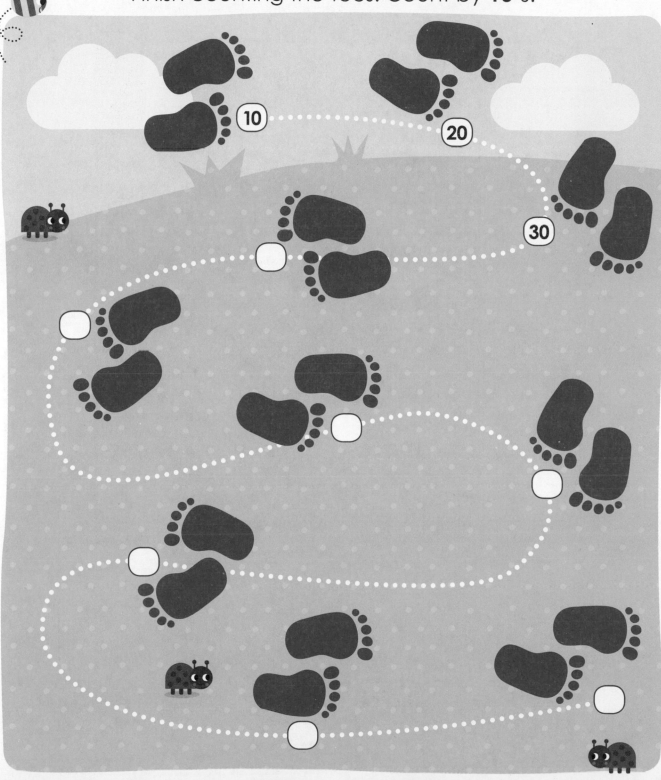

Skip counting by 10's

Use a **red** pencil to finish skip counting by **10**'s up to 100.

1	2	3	4	5	6	7	8	9	10
11	12	13	14	15	16	17	18	19	20
21	22	23	24	25	26	27	28	29	30
31	32	33	34	35	36	37	38	39	40
41	42	43	44	45	46	47	48	49	50
51	52	53	54	55	56	57	58	59	60
61	62	63	64	65	66	67	68	69	70
71	72	73	74	75	76	77	78	79	80
81	82	83	84	85	86	87	88	89	90
91	92	93	94	95	96	97	98	99	100

COUNTING TO 100

Counting

Fill in the numbers on the caterpillars.

4 5 6 _ _ 9 _ _

16 17 _ _ _ _ 22 _

43 44 _ _ _ 48 _ _

68 69 _ _ _ 72 _ _

77 78 _ _ _ _ 83 _

92 93 94 95 _ _ _ 99

Counting back

Fill in the numbers on the trains. Count down.

| 10 | 9 | 8 | | | | | |

| 20 | 19 | | 17 | | | | |

| 40 | | | 37 | | | | |

| 55 | 54 | | | | | | |

| 82 | | | | | 77 | | |

| 100 | | | | | | | 93 |

Count to 100

Now you can count to 100!
Write the numbers in the hundred chart.

			3						
									20
				25					
							38		
42									
		54							
61									
						77			
				86					
								99	

Follow the I's

Color the **1**'s to guide the hen to her chick.

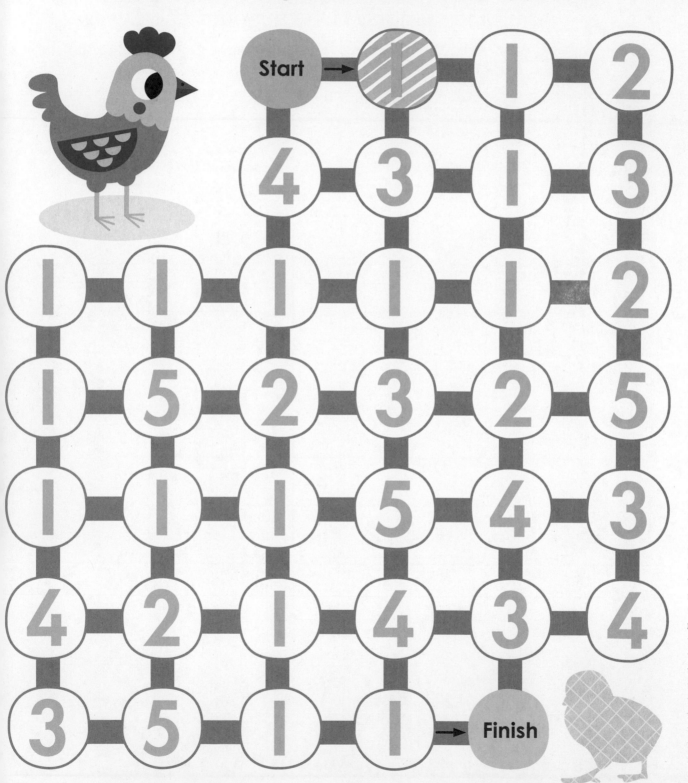

Find the 2's

Color the parrot. Then trace a path to the pineapples.
You can only pass through the groups of **2**.

Follow the 3's

Color the **3**'s to guide the rocket to the planet.

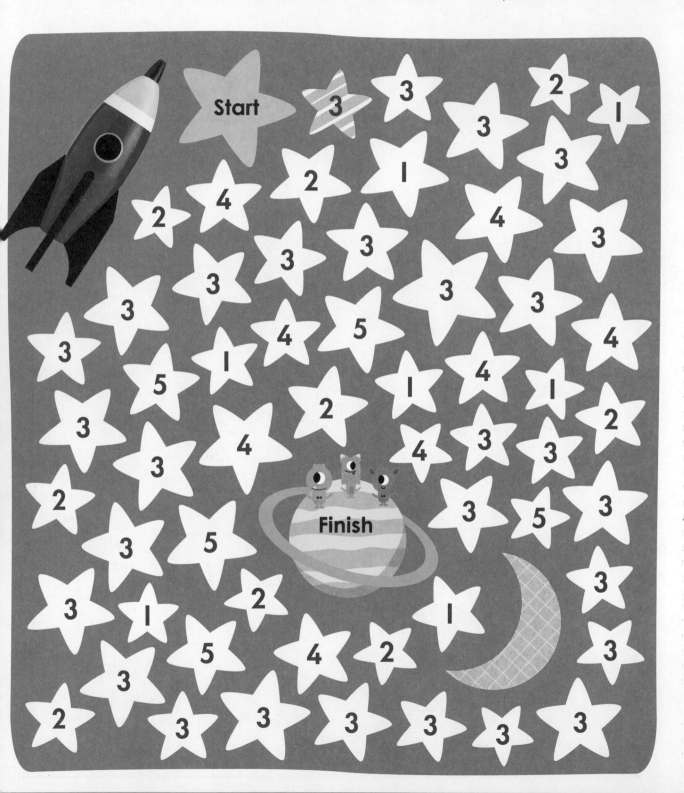

Follow the 4's

Color the **4**'s to guide the mouse to the cheese.

Start	4	4	1	2
	3	5	4	4	6
2	6	9	5	7	8	4	7
5	7	8	4	4	4	4	5
8	4	4	4	8	9	2	5
1	4	7	6	2	6	1	8
3	4	4	2	1	7	9	3
2	9	4	4	4	9	Finish
8	7	1	5	4	4	

169

Count to 5

Trace a path from **1** to **5** to find the group of **5** butterflies.

Follow the 10's

Follow the **10**'s to help the monkey reach the bananas.

Start

10	10	10	
10	10	10	10
10	10	3	6	7
2	10			2
4	10			5
9	10			8
8	10	7	4	2
10	10	3	8	9
10	10	10	10	10

Finish

From 1 to 10

Trace a path from **1** to **10** past the race cars to reach the finish line.

Start

Finish

From 10 to 20

Follow the numbers from **10** to **20** to help the family reach the park.

Start → 10 16 10

11 12 18

18 16 15 15 14 13 11

19 20 16 11 18 15

10 12 18 17 12

11 12 19 20 → Finish 11

Count to 20

Follow the numbers from **1** to **20**
to help the frog across the lily pads.

Start

Finish

Skip counting by 5's

Skip count by **5**'s to reach **50**. Color the spaces as you go.

| 6 | 14 | 3 | **5** Start |
| 18 | 15 | 10 | |

12 20

28

24 25 37

30

35 32

33

40

50 Finish 45 42

49

Even numbers to 20

Follow the **even numbers** in order
to help the children find the exit.

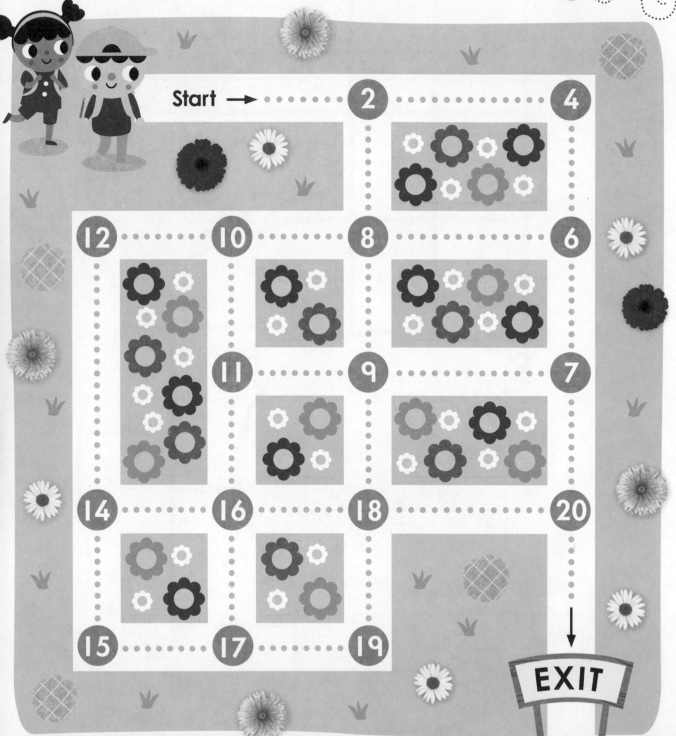

Start → 2 4

12 10 8 6

11 9 7

14 16 18 20

15 17 19

EXIT

Odd numbers to 20

Follow the **odd numbers** in order through the rainbow maze.

5

9

7

6

11

3

2

15

13

4

16

17

8

1

12

19 14

Start

Finish

Skip counting by 10's

Skip count by **10**'s to guide the farmer to the barn. Color the spaces as you go.

Start → 10

18

20

15

25

64

40

30

50

33

70

60

45

80

77

82

99

90

100

Finish

The ones place

Ones are digits that stand for numbers between **0** and **9**. In the number **34**, **4** is in the **ones place**.

Follow the numbers with **9** in the **ones place** to help the kangaroo reach her joey.

Start

9	19	15	18	13
20	29	35	57	44
41	23	39	49	59	67
43	88	36	70	69	75
56	72	82	89	79	84
92	96	93	99		
98	83	57	100	

Finish

Follow the path

Follow the instructions to find a path through the fish's scales.

Color the numbers with **2** in the **ones place** in **blue**.
Color the numbers with **5** in the **ones place** in **green**.
Color the numbers with **8** in the **ones place** in **pink**.

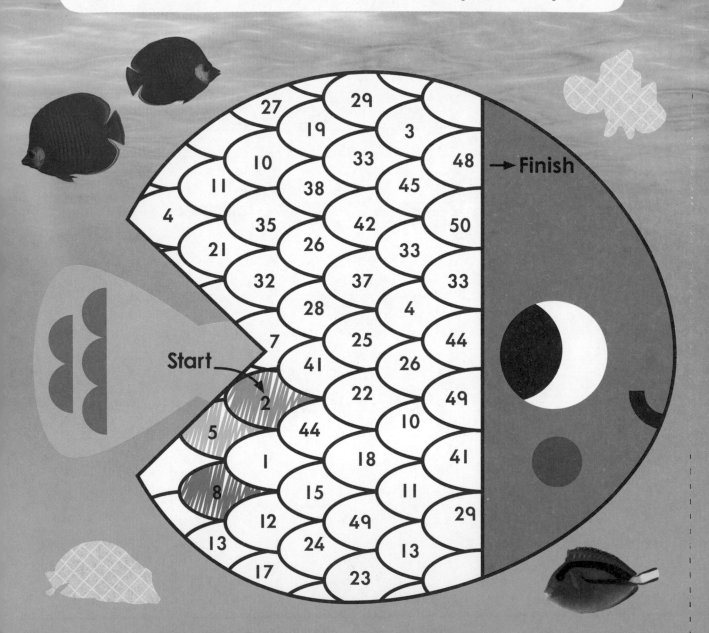

Finish

Start

The tens place

Tens are digits that stand for 10, 20, 30, 40, 50, 60, 70, 80, or 90.
In the number **34**, **3** is in the **tens place**. It stands for **30**.

Follow the numbers with **6** in the **tens place**
to help the owl reach its nest.

66
67
65
56
68
69
Finish
26
56
64
63
36
93
20
62
57
Start → 61
86
16
36

Unicorn maze

Find your way through the unicorn's maze.
Color the numbers with **7** in the **ones place purple**.

Monster maze

Find your way through the monster's maze.
Color the numbers with **1** in the **tens place** yellow.
Also color the numbers with **0** in the **ones place** yellow.

78	18	100	17	80	16	70	15	68	67
58	10	96	82	83	74	64	60	52	45
46	19	97			72	29	14	50	13
36	20	99			22	25	33	36	40
21	11	86	**Start**		10	20	11	30	12
53	30	87	75	64	23	26	37	39	42
40	12	72	70	17	80	86	79	99	89
13	38	29	16	22	18	93	83		
50	14	60	15	49	90	19	100		**Finish**

Ten frame addition

Here is **1 pink button** and **1 orange button**. How many buttons are there altogether?

1 + 1 = 2

Here are 2 blue cars and **1 red car**. How many cars are there altogether?

2 + 1 = ◯

Here are **3 purple socks** and **1 brown sock**. How many socks are there altogether?

3 + 1 = ◯

Here are 4 green leaves and 1 yellow leaf. How many leaves are there altogether?

4 + 1 = ◯

Ten frame subtraction

Here are **4 fish**.
Cross out **1 fish**.
How many are left?

4 – 1 = ③

Here are **6 guitars**.
Cross out **1 guitar**.
How many are left?

6 – 1 = ◯

Here are **8 chicks**.
Cross out **1 chick**.
How many are left?

8 – 1 = ◯

Here is **1 dog**.
Cross out **1 dog**.
How many are left?

1 – 1 = ◯

Add 1

Draw pictures to help you solve the problems.

Draw 1 more ball.

$2 + 1 = \bigcirc$

Draw 1 more T-shirt.

$3 + 1 = \bigcirc$

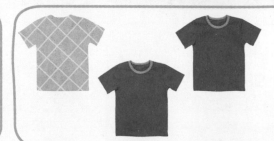

Draw 1 more bee.

$5 + 1 = \bigcirc$

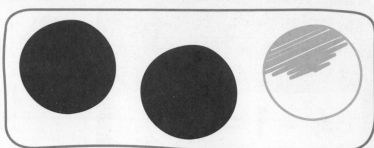

Draw 1 more cookie.

$6 + 1 = \bigcirc$

Draw 1 more heart.

$8 + 1 = \bigcirc$

Subtract 1

Cross out **1** from each box to solve the problem.

Cross out **1 beetle**.

$$2 - 1 = \bigcirc$$

Cross out **1 digger**.

$$3 - 1 = \bigcirc$$

Cross out **1 rabbit**.

$$5 - 1 = \bigcirc$$

Cross out **1 flower**.

$$8 - 1 = \bigcirc$$

Cross out **1 hat**.

$$10 - 1 = \bigcirc$$

Add 2

Count on from **2** to solve the problems.

2 + 1 = ◯

2 + 2 = ◯

2 + 3 = ◯

2 + 4 = ◯

2 + 5 = ◯

2 + 6 = ◯

2 + 7 = ◯

2 + 8 = ◯

Subtract 2

Cross out **2** from each box to solve the problem.

3 − 2 = ◯

4 − 2 = ◯

5 − 2 = ◯

6 − 2 = ◯

7 − 2 = ◯

8 − 2 = ◯

9 − 2 = ◯

10 − 2 = ◯

Add 3

Count on from **3** to solve the problems.

3 + 1 = ◯

3 + 2 = ◯

3 + 3 = ◯

3 + 4 = ◯

3 + 5 = ◯

3 + 6 = ◯

3 + 7 = ◯

Subtract 3

Cross out **3** from each box to solve the problem.

4 − 3 = ◯

5 − 3 = ◯

6 − 3 = ◯

7 − 3 = ◯

8 − 3 = ◯

9 − 3 = ◯

10 − 3 = ◯

Add 4

Count on from **4** to solve the problems.

4 + 1 = ◯

4 + 2 = ◯

4 + 3 = ◯

4 + 4 = ◯

4 + 5 = ◯

4 + 6 = ◯

Four tractors meet **four** more tractors.

How many tractors are there now? ◯

Subtract 4

Cross out **4** from each box to solve the problem.

5 – 4 = ◯

6 – 4 = ◯

7 – 4 = ◯

8 – 4 = ◯

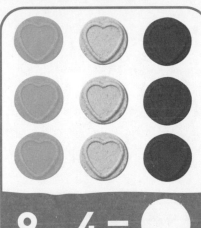

9 – 4 = ◯

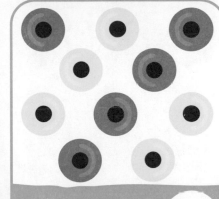

10 – 4 = ◯

Six children were skipping. **Four** had to go home.

How many children are left? ◯

Add 5

Count on from **5** to solve the problems.

5 + 0 = ◯

5 + 1 = ◯

5 + 2 = ◯

5 + 3 = ◯

5 + 4 = ◯

5 + 5 = ◯

Five girls go to school, and so do **five** boys.

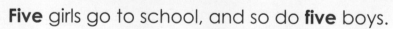

How many children go to school altogether? ◯

Subtract 5

Cross out **5** from each box to solve the problem.

$5 - 5 =$ ◯

$6 - 5 =$ ◯

$7 - 5 =$ ◯

$8 - 5 =$ ◯

$9 - 5 =$ ◯

$10 - 5 =$ ◯

Six puppies were playing. **Five** fell asleep.

How many puppies are still playing? ◯

Adding by 2's ★

Count by **2**'s to figure out how many children there are.

two **four** **six** **eight** **ten**

2 + 2 + 2 + 2 + 2 = ◯

Count by **2**'s to figure out how many socks there are.

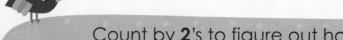

two **four** **six** **eight** **ten**

twelve **fourteen** **sixteen** **eighteen** **twenty**

2 + 2 + 2 + 2 + 2 + 2 + 2 + 2 + 2 + 2 = ◯

★ ★ Adding by 5's

Count by **5**'s to figure out how many fingers there are.

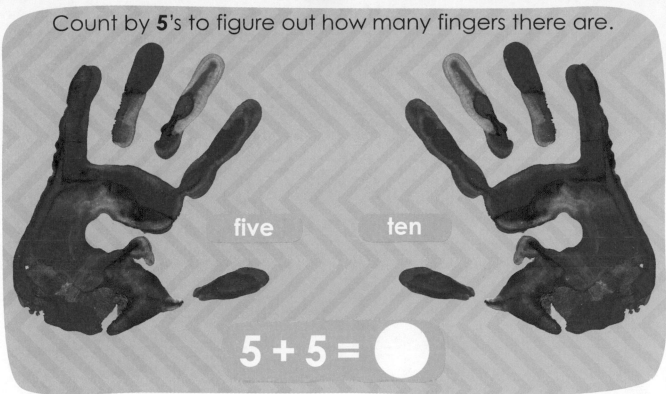

five ten

$5 + 5 = \bigcirc$

Count by **5**'s to figure out how many flowers there are.

five ten fifteen twenty

$5 + 5 + 5 + 5 = \bigcirc$

Adding to 20

Count on from **10** to solve the problems.

10 + 1 = ◯

10 + 2 = ◯

10 + 3 = ◯

10 + 4 = ◯

10 + 5 = ◯

Adding to 20

Count on from **10** to solve the problems.

10 + 6 = ◯

10 + 7 = ◯

10 + 8 = ◯

10 + 9 = ◯

10 + 10 = ◯

199

Subtracting from 20

Cross out cars to help you solve the problems.

20 − 1 = ◯

20 − 2 = ◯

20 − 3 = ◯

20 − 4 = ◯

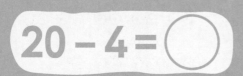

20 − 5 = ◯

Subtracting from 20

Cross out fish to help you solve the problems.

20 – 6 = ◯

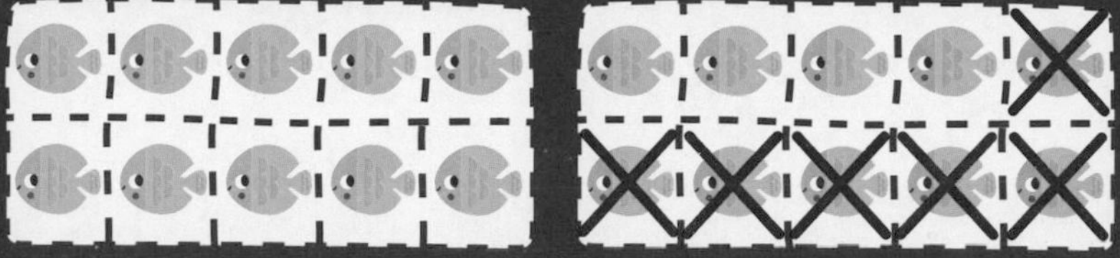

20 – 7 = ◯

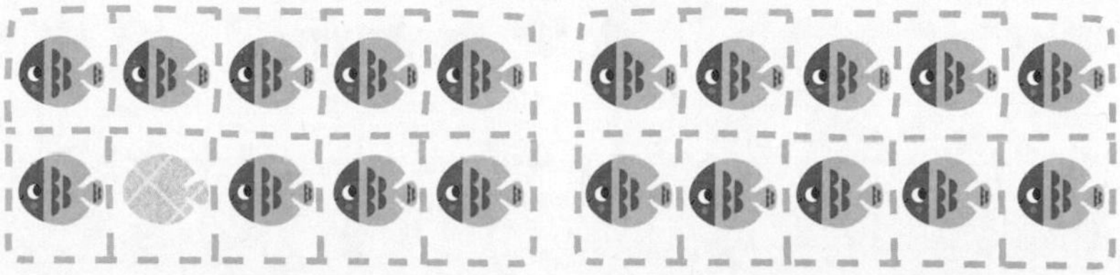

20 – 8 = ◯

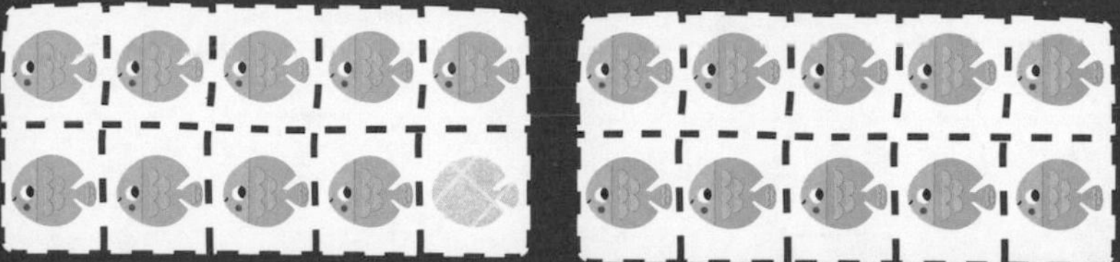

20 – 9 = ◯

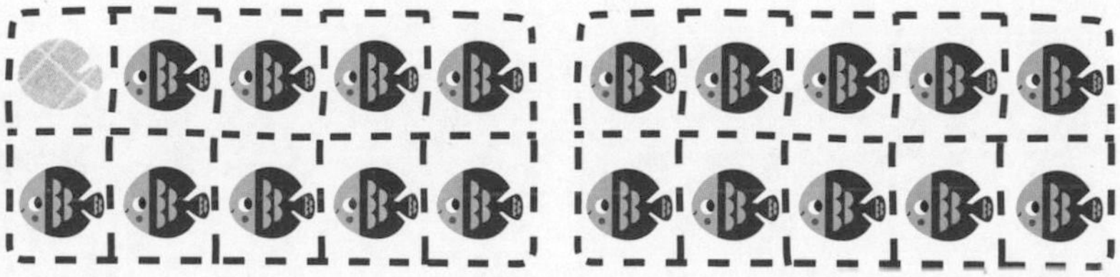

20 –10 = ◯

★ Count by tens

Count by **10**'s to figure out how many stars there are.

 + = **20** stars

+ + = ◯ stars

+ + + + = ◯ stars

+ + + + + = ◯ stars

+ + + + + + = ◯ stars

+ + + + + + + + = ◯ stars

Subtract tens

Cross out groups of **10** to solve the problems.

$40 - 20 =$ **20**

$50 - 20 =$ ◯

$60 - 30 =$ ◯

$60 - 40 =$ ◯

$80 - 30 =$ ◯

$100 - 50 =$ ◯

Match the shapes

Draw lines to match the **shapes**.

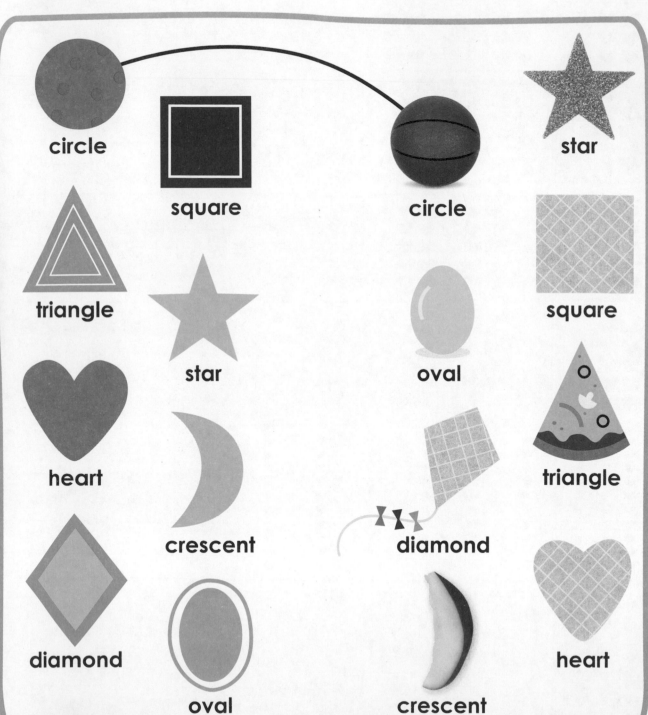

circle

square

circle

star

triangle

star

oval

square

heart

crescent

oval

diamond

diamond

triangle

heart

crescent

How many sides?

How many **sides** does each shape have?
Draw lines to link the **numbers** to the **shapes**.

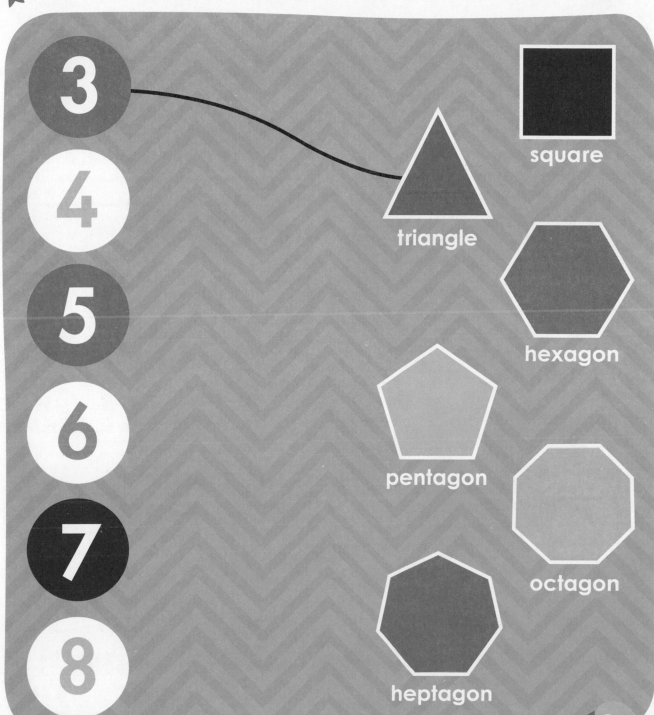

3

4

5

6

7

8

square

triangle

hexagon

pentagon

octagon

heptagon

205

Count the sides

Use the key to color the **shapes**.

3 sides = blue   **4 sides** = orange

5 sides = green   **6 sides** = red

How many **shapes** have **4 sides**? ......

Count the corners

Some **shapes** have **corners**.
Count the **corners** and write the **number**.

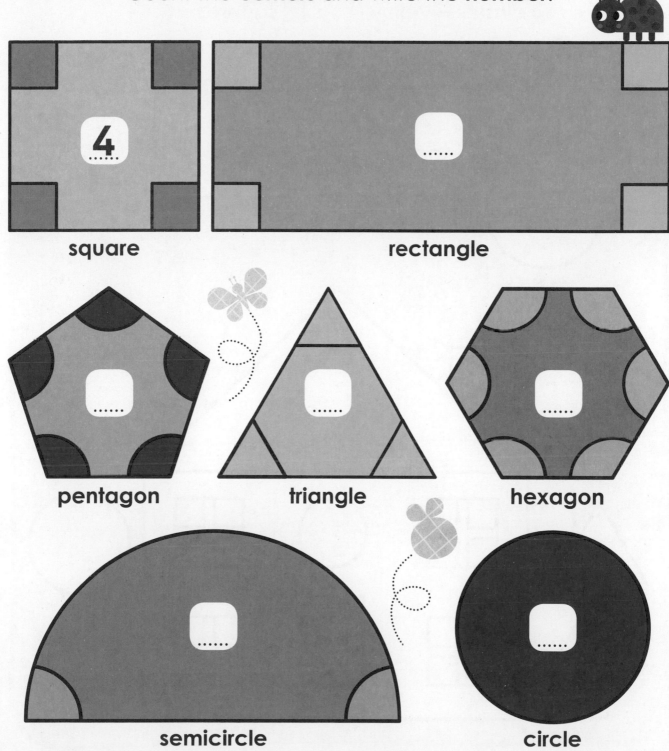

square 4

rectangle ......

pentagon ......

triangle ......

hexagon ......

semicircle ......

circle ......

Shape art

Use the color key to finish coloring the picture.

● **circles = yellow**   ■ **squares = blue**

▬ **rectangles = orange**   ▲ **triangles = red**

2-D and 3-D

Draw lines to match the **2-D** and **3-D shapes**.

circle

cuboid

sphere

triangle

rectangle

cube

square

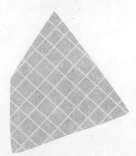
triangle-based
pyramid

3-D shapes

Draw lines to match the **3-D shapes**.

cube

cone

cube

cone

sphere

square-based
pyramid

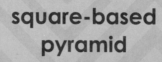

square-based
pyramid

cylinder

cylinder

sphere

Make a dice

You will need:

 safety scissors

 clear tape

 light cardboard

counters

dice

Instructions:

1 Carefully remove this page and glue it onto a piece of cardboard.

2 When the glue is dry, ask an adult to cut out the counters and the dice along the thick blue edges.

3 Fold the dice along the dashed lines to make a cube.

rectangle

triangle   circle   square   star

diamond

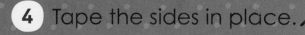

4 Tape the sides in place.

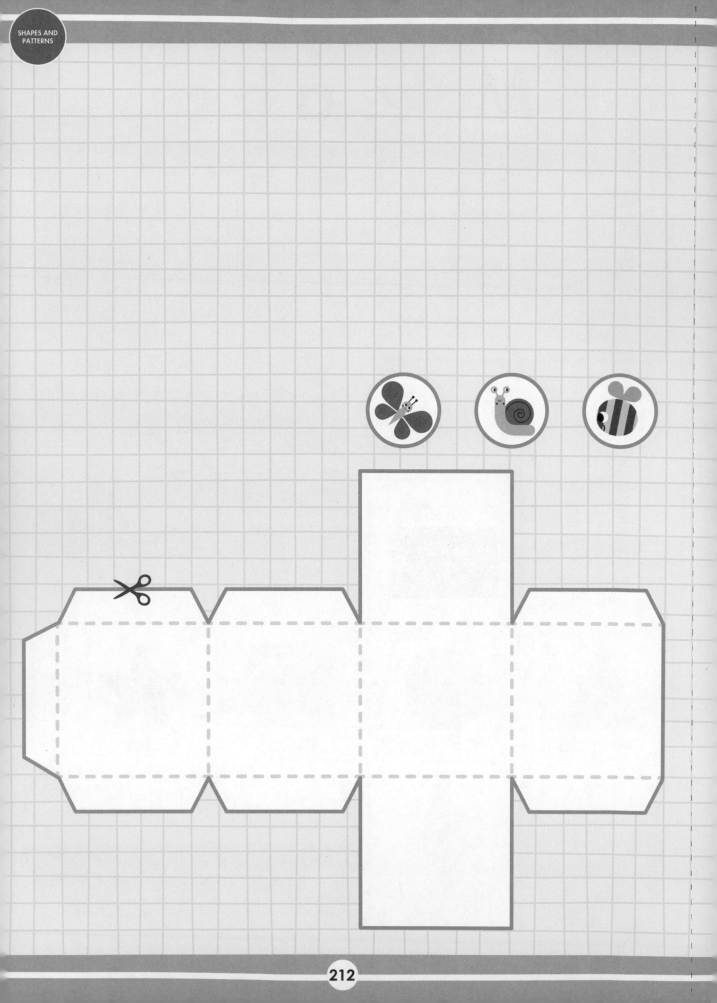

Patterns we wear

Match the **patterns** to the ones the children are wearing.

stripes

checks

polka dots

Shapes game

Use your dice and counters
from page 211 to play this game.

Instructions:

1. Place your counter on the start space. Then take turns rolling the dice.

2. When it is your turn, move your counter along the board until you reach the shape on the top of the dice.

3. The first person to reach the finish box is the winner.

Start →

Finish

Look at patterns

How many different **pictures** make up each **pattern**?

1

What comes next?

Draw what comes next in each row.

Make up a **pattern** of your own here.

Brick patterns

What **shape** makes up this wall?
Circle the answer.

triangles   **hexagons**   **rectangles**

Finish coloring these bricks in the same **pattern**.

How many **sides** does each brick have? ......

Bees make patterns

 What **shape** makes up honeycomb?
Circle the answer.

triangles   hexagons   rectangles

Finish coloring this honeycomb in the same **pattern**.

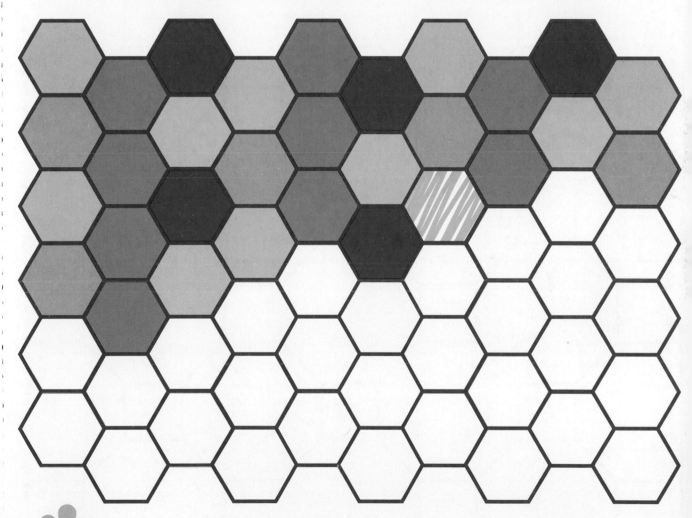

How many **sides** does each shape have? ......

Mosaic 1

Shapes fit together to make **patterns**.
Color each **shape** a different color.

Mosaic ②

Color each **shape** a different color.

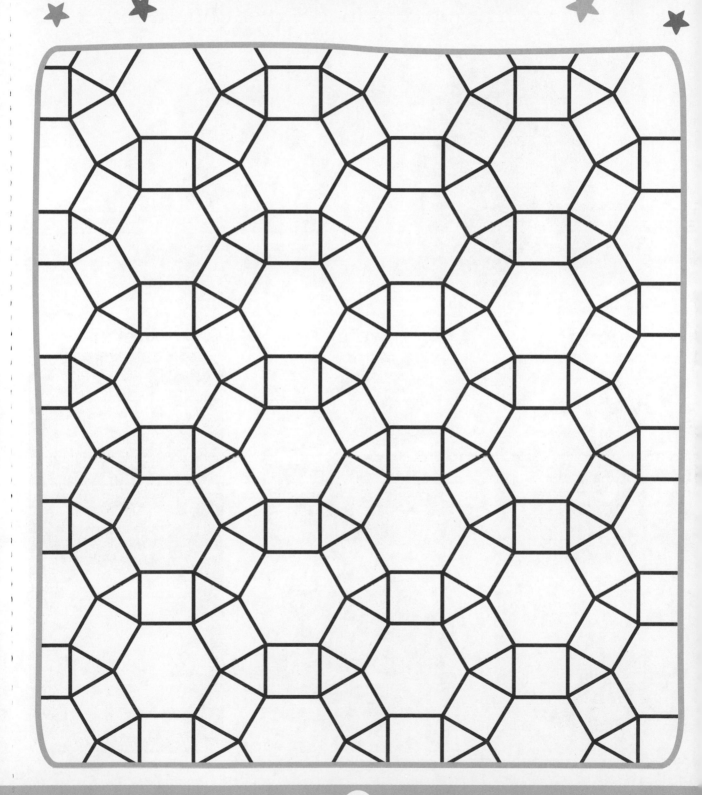

What animals need

Animals need **food**, **water**, and **shelter**. Draw a different line from each animal to its food, water, and shelter.

food

water

shelter

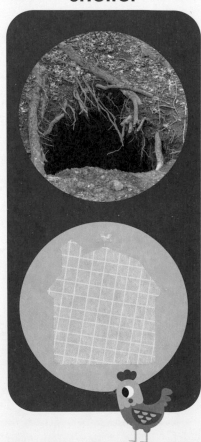

What plants need

Plants need **water** and **sunshine**.
Put a check by the plants that will live and grow.
Put a cross by the plants that will die.

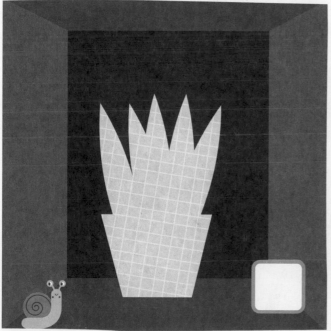

Insects

Most **insects** have the same body parts.
Look at the **bee** diagram. Then draw lines to join the
orange labels to the correct parts on the **dragonfly**.

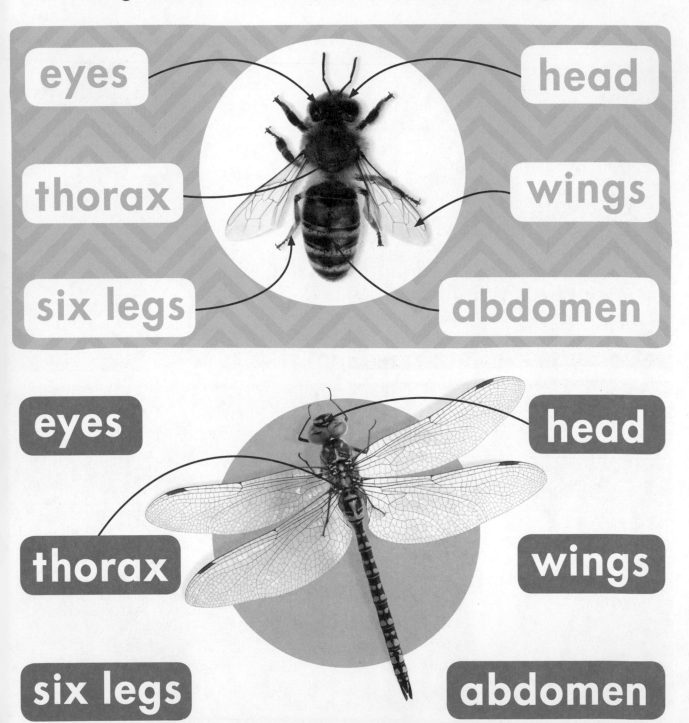

eyes

head

thorax

wings

six legs

abdomen

eyes

head

thorax

wings

six legs

abdomen

Fish

Look at the labels on the **goldfish**.
Write the same labels on the **tropical fish**.

fins

eye

scales

mouth

tail

Amphibians

Trace and read these **amphibian** names.

 **newt**  **frog**  **toad**

Amphibians spend part of their lives **in water** and part **on land**.
Add the label stickers to this frog life-cycle diagram.

Reptiles

Trace and read these **reptile** names.

crocodile

snake

turtle

lizard

Use the pictures to help match the sentence **beginnings** and **endings**.

snake

skink

All reptiles have	are reptiles.
Some reptiles don't	have any legs.
Snakes and skinks	scaly skin.

Birds

Trace and read these **bird** names.

parrot  seagull

pigeon  jay

Use the pictures to help decide if each sentence is true or false.

hummingbird

ostrich

All birds have feathers.	(true) / false
All birds are the same size.	true / false
All birds can fly.	true / false
All birds have beaks.	true / false

Mammals

Sticker the missing words into the sentences.

Mammals have ⬚⬚⬚ or hair on their bodies.

Mammals feed their babies ⬚⬚⬚ .

Dogs, lions, mice, and pigs are all ⬚⬚⬚ .

Circle the animals that are **mammals**.

My body

Write and sticker labels on the diagram.
Words to write: **leg arm foot eye**

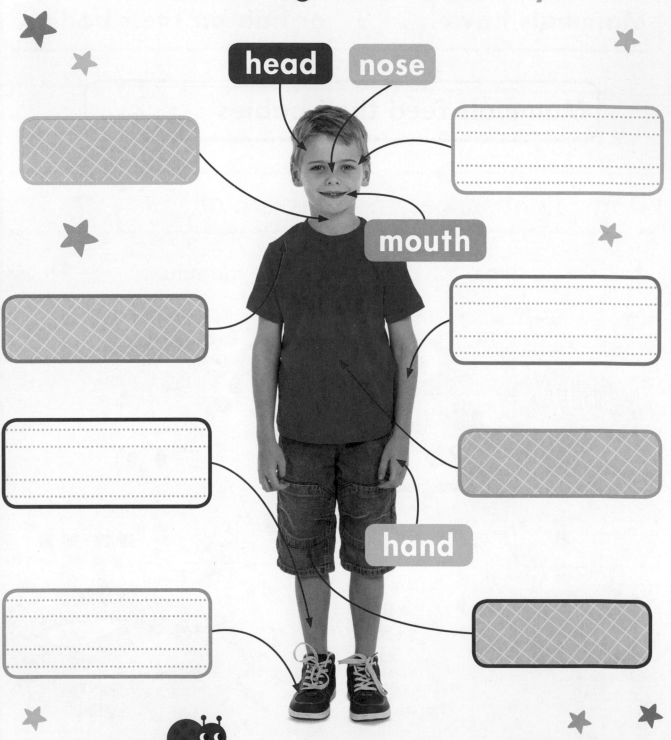

head   **nose**

mouth

hand

Five senses

Trace the five **sense words**.
Then draw lines to match them to the pictures.

touch

see

hear

smell

taste

Energy

Plants, animals, and people need **energy** to **move** and **grow**. Machines need **energy** to **work**. Draw a line to join each thing with its energy source.

 flashlight

 electric wires

 cow

electric batteries

bear

fish

 people

gas

 refrigerator

food

 car

grass

Movement, heat, or light

Machines use energy to make **heat**, **light**, or **movement**.
Draw lines to match each machine with the correct word.

heat

move

light

Reflections

Your image in a mirror is a **reflection**.
Reflections happen when light bounces off a smooth surface.
Find and circle the **reflections** in these pictures.

It's see-through

Light can go through some things.
These things are **see-through**.
Circle the things that are **see-through**, or **transparent**.

Fast and slow

Circle the **fast** things in green.
Circle the **slow** things in red.

Circle the things that are **getting faster** in orange.
Circle the things that are **getting slower** in blue.

Push and pull

Draw lines to match each action with the correct word.

pull

push

SCIENCE

Friction

It is easy to move on **smooth** surfaces, but they are **slippery**.
It is harder to move on **rough** surfaces, but they are **not slippery**.
Draw lines to join the pictures with the correct words.

smooth and
slippery

rough and
not slippery

Tools

Match the tools with the tasks they help us do.

telescope

measuring cup

height chart

magnifying glass

thermometer

scale

see stars better

find out how tall I am

find out how heavy it is

find out if I have a fever

look at bugs close up

MILK

find out how much I have

Congratulations!

GOOD WORK AWARD!

Name: ....

has successfully completed the

Kindergarten

Jumbo Workbook

Date: ....